The land of the blue flower

Frances Hodgson Burnett, William James Jordan, Plimpton Press, Sigismund De Ivanowski

THE LAND OF THE BLUE FLOWER

From a Painting by Sigismond de Ivanowski

"There is no time for anger"

THE LAND OF THE BLUE FLOWER

BY

FRANCES HODGSON BURNETT

WITH A FRONTISPIECE
BY
SIGISMOND DE IVANOWSKI

NEW YORK
MOFFAT, YARD AND COMPANY
1909

PUBLISHED, SEPTEMBER, 1909

The Plimpton Press Norwood Mass. U.S.A.

PART I

PART I

THE Land of the Blue Flower was not called by that name until the tall, strong, beautiful King Amor came down from his castle on the mountain crag and began to reign. Before that time it was called King Mordreth's Land, and as the first King Mordreth had been a fierce and cruel king this seemed a gloomy name.

A few weeks before Amor was born, his weak, selfish boy-father — whose name was King Mordreth also — had been killed while hunting, and his fair mother with the clear eyes died when he was but a few hours old. But early in that day she sent for her venerable friend and teacher, who was said to be the oldest and wisest man in the world, and who long ago had fled to a cave in the mountains, that he might see no more of the famine and disorder and hatred in the country spread out on the plains below.

He was a marvelous old man, almost a giant in size, and having great blue eyes like deep sea-water. They, too, were clear eyes like the fair Queen's — they seemed to see all things and to hold in their depths no single thought which was not fine and great. The people were a little afraid of him when they saw him go striding majestically through their streets. They had no name for him but The Ancient One.

The lovely Queen drew aside the embroidered coverlet of her gold and ivory bed and showed him the tiny baby sleeping by her side.

"He was born a King," she said. "No one can help him but you."

The Ancient One looked down at him.

"He has long limbs and strong ones. He will make a great King," he said. "Give him to me."

The Queen held out the little new-born one in her arms.

"Take him away quickly before he hears the people quarreling at the palace gate," she said. "Take him to the castle on the mountain crag. Keep him there until he is old enough to come down and be King. When the sun sinks behind the clouds I shall die, but if he is with you he will learn what Kings should know."

The Ancient One took the child, folded him in his long gray robe and strode majestically through the palace gates, through the ugly city and out over the plains to the mountain. When he began to climb its steep sides the sun was setting and casting a golden rose color over the big rocks and the wild flowers and bushes which grew on every side, so that there seemed no path to be found. But the Ancient One knew his way anywhere in the world without a path to guide him. He climbed and climbed, and little King Amor slept soundly in the folds of his gray robe. He reached the summit at last and pushing his way through a jungle of twisted vines starred all over with pale sweet-scented buds, he stood looking at the castle which was set on the very topmost crag, and looked out over the mountain's edge at the sea and the sky and the spreading plains below.

The sky was dark blue now and lit by a myriad stars, and all was so still that the world seemed thousands of miles away, and ugliness and squalor and people who quarreled seemed things which were not true. A sweet cool wind blew about them as the Ancient One took King Amor from the folds of his gray robe and laid him on the carpet of scented moss.

"The stars are very near," he said. "Waken, young King, and see how near they are and know they are your brothers. Your brother the wind is bringing to you the breath of your brothers the trees. You are at home."

Then King Amor opened his eyes, and when he saw the stars in the dark blueness above him he smiled, and though he was not yet a whole day old he threw up his small hand and it touched his forehead.

"Like a King and a soldier he salutes them," said the Ancient One; "though he does not know he did it."

The castle was huge and splendid though it had been deserted for a hundred years. For three generations the royal owners had not cared to look out on the world from high places. They knew nothing of the wind and the trees and the stars; they lived on the plains in their cities, and hunted and rioted and levied heavy taxes on their wretched people. And the castle had lived through its summers and winters alone. It had battlements and towers which stood out clear against the sky, and there was a great banquet hall and chambers for hundreds of guests, and rooms for a thousand men at arms, and the courtyard was big enough to hold a tournament in.

In the midst of its space and splendor the little King Amor lived alone but for the companionship of the Ancient One and a servant as old as himself. But they knew a secret which had kept them young in spite of the years they had passed through. They knew that they were the brothers of all things in the world, and that the man who never knows an angered or evil thought can never know a foe. They were strong and straight and wise, and the wildest creature stopped to give them greeting as it passed, and they understood its language when it spoke. Because they held no dark thoughts in their minds they knew no fear, and because they knew no fear the wild creatures knew none and the speech of each was clear to the other.

Each morning they went out on the battlements at dawn to see the splendid sun rise slowly out of the purple sea. One of the very first things the child King Amor remembered in his life — and he remembered it always — was a dawning day when the Ancient One wakened him gently, and folding him in his long gray robe carried him up the winding and narrow stone stairway, until at last they stepped forth on the top of the huge castle which seemed to the little creature to be so high that it was quite close to the wonderful sky itself.

"The sun is going to rise and wake the world," said the Ancient One. "Young King, watch the wonder of it."

Amor lifted his little head and looked. He was only just old enough to be beginning to understand things, but he loved the Ancient One and all he said and did.

Far below the mountain crag lay the sea. In the night, while it slept, it had looked dark blue or violet, but now it was slowly changing its color. The sky was changing too — it was growing paler and paler — next it grew faintly brighter, so did the sea; then a slight flush crept over land and water and all the small floating clouds were rosy pink. King Amor smiled because birds' voices were to be heard in the trees and bushes, and something golden bright was rising out of the edge of the ocean, and sparkling light danced on the waves. It rose higher and higher and grew so dazzling and wonderful that he threw out his little hand with a shout of joy. The next moment he started back because there rose near him a loud whirr and beating of powerful wings as a great bird flew out of a crag near by and soared high into the radiant morning heavens.

"It is the eagle who is our neighbor," said the Ancient One. "He has awakened and gone to give his greeting to the sun."

And as the little King sat upright, enraptured, he saw that from the dazzling brightness at the edge of the world there leaped forth a ball of living gold and fire, and even he knew that the sun had risen.

"At every day's dawn it leaps forth like that," said the Ancient One. "Let us watch together and I will tell you stories of it."

So they sat by the battlement and the stories were told. They were stories of the small grains lying hid in the dark earth waiting for the golden heat of the sun to draw them forth into life until they covered the tilled fields with waving wheat to make bread for the world; they were stories of the seeds of fair flowers warmed and ripened until they burst into scented blossoms; they were stories of the roots of trees and the rich sap drawn upward by the heat until great branches and thick leafage waved in the summer air; they were stories of men, women, and children walking with light step and glad because of the gold of the sun.

"Every day it warms, every day it draws, every day it ripens and gives life. And there are many who forget the wonder of it. Lift your head high as you walk, young King, and often look upward. Never forget the sun."

At every dawning they rose and saw together the wonder of the day; and the first time the sky was heavy with gray clouds and the sun did not leap upward from behind the edge of the world the Ancient One said another thing.

"The burning gold is behind the

lowering gray and purple. The clouds are heavy with soft rain. When they break they will drop it in showers or splendid storms and the thirsty earth will drink it up. The grains will drink it and the seed and the roots, and the world will be joyous and rich with fresh life; the springs will bubble up like crystal, and the brooks will rush babbling through the green of the forest. The drinking places for the cattle will be full and clear and men and women will feel rested and cool. Lift your head high when you walk, young King, and often look upward. Never forget the clouds."

So hearing these things every day King Amor learned the meaning of both sun and cloud and loved and felt himself brother to both.

The first time he remembered seeing a storm the Ancient One took him to the battlements again, and together they watched the dark clouds pour down their floods while their purple was riven by the dazzling lances of the lightning; and the thunder rolled and crashed and seemed to rend asunder things no human eye could see; and the wind roared round the castle on the mountain crag and beat against its towers, and tossed the branches of the hugest trees, and whirled the rain in sheets over the land, — and King Amor stood erect and strong like some little soldier, though he wondered where the small birds were and if the eagle were in his nest.

Through all the tumult the Ancient One stood still. He looked taller than ever in his long gray robe, and his strange eyes were deep as the sea.

At last he said in a slow, calm voice: "This is the voice of the power men know not. No man has yet quite understood — though it seems to speak. Harken to it. Let your soul stand silent. Listen, young King. Hold your head high as you walk and often look upward. Never forget the storm."

So the King learned to love the storm and be one with it, knowing no fear.

But perhaps — it might be because he had been laid on the scented moss and had without knowing it saluted them on the first night of his life — he felt nearest to, and loved most, his brothers the stars.

Every fair night through the King's earliest years the Ancient One carried him to the battlements and let him fall asleep beneath the shining myriads. But first he would walk about bearing him in his arms, or sit with him in the splendid silence, sometimes relating wonders to him in a low voice, sometimes uttering no word, only looking calmly into the high vault above as if the stars spoke to him and told him of perfect peace.

"When a man looks long at them," he said, "he grows calm and forgets small things. They answer his questions and show him that his earth is only one of the million worlds. Hold your soul still and look upward often, and you will understand their speech. Never forget the stars."

PART II

PART II

SO, as the child King grew day by day, the world seemed to grow fuller and fuller of wonders and beauties. There were the sun and the moon, the storm and the stars, the straight falling lances of rain, the springing of the growing things, the flight of the eagle, the songs and nests of small bird creatures, the changing seasons, and the work of the great brown earth giving its harvest and its fruits.

"All these wonders in one world and you a man upon it," said the Ancient One. "Hold high your head when you walk, young King, and often look upward. Never forget one marvel among them all."

He forgot nothing. He lived looking out on all things from great, clear, joyous eyes. Upon his mountain crag he never heard a paltry or unbeautiful word or knew of the existence of unfriendliness or baseness in thought. As soon as he was old enough to go out alone he roamed about the great mountain and feared neither storm nor wild beasts. Shaggy-maned lions and their mates drew near and fawned on him as their kind had fawned on young Adam in the Garden of Eden. There had never passed through his mind the thought that they were not his friends. He did not know that there were men who killed their wild brothers.

In the huge courtyard of the castle

he learned to ride and to perform great feats of strength. Because he had not learned to be afraid he never feared that he could not do a thing. He grew so strong and beautiful that when he was ten years old he was as tall as a youth of sixteen, and when he was sixteen he was already like a young giant. This was because he had been brother to the storm and had lived close to the strength and splendor of the stars.

Only once, when he was a boy of twelve, a strange and painful thing happened to him. From his kingdom in the plains below there had been sent to him a beautiful young horse which had been bred for him. Never had so magnificent an animal been born in the royal stable. When he was brought into the courtyard the boy King's eyes shone with joy. He spent the greater part of the morning in exercising and leaping him over barriers. The Ancient One in his tower chamber heard his shouts of exultation and encouragement. At last the King went out to try him on the winding mountain road.

When he returned he went at once to the tower chamber to the Ancient One, who, when he raised his eyes from his great book, looked at him gravely.

"Let us climb to the battlements," the boy said. "We must talk together."

So they went, and when they stood looking out on the world below, the curving turquoise sky above them, the eyes of the Ancient One were still more grave.

"Tell me, young King."

"Something strange has happened," King Amor answered. "I have felt something I have not felt before. I was riding my horse around the field on the plateau and he saw something which he refused to pass. It was a young leopard watching us from a tree. My horse reared and snorted. He would not listen to me, but backed and wheeled around. I tried in vain to persuade him, and suddenly, when I saw I could not make him obey me, this strange new feeling rushed through all my body. I grew hot and knew my face was scarlet, my heart beat faster and my blood seemed to boil in my veins. I shouted out harsh, ugly sounds — I forgot that all things are brothers — I lifted my hand and clenched it and struck my horse again and again. I loved him no longer, I felt that he no longer loved me. I am hot and wearied and heavy from it still. I feel no more joy. Was it pain I felt? I have never felt pain and do not know. Was it pain?"

"It was a worse thing," answered the Ancient One. "It was anger. When a man is overcome by anger he has a poisoned fever. He loses his strength, he loses his power over himself and over others, he throws away time in which he might have gained the end he most desires. *There is no time for anger in the world.*"

So King Amor learned the uselessness of anger, for they sat long upon the battlements while the Ancient One told him how its poison worked in the veins and weakened the strongest man until he was made a fool. That night Amor lay under the sky looking at his myriad brothers, the stars, and drawing calm from them.

"If you lie through the night upon the battlements and think only of the stillness and the stars you will forget your anger and its poison will die away. If you put into your mind a beautiful thought it will take the place of the evil one. There is no room for darkness in the mind of him who thinks only of the stars." This had been said to him by the Ancient One.

Upon the plateau at the foot of the crag on which the castle stood there were marvelous walled gardens. The sad young Queen of the first King Mordreth had planted them, and after her death they had been left to run wild. Since the baby King Amor had been brought to the mountain top the Ancient One and his servitor had made them bloom again. As soon as he was old enough to hold a small spade Amor had worked in the beds. All things grew for him as if his touch were a spell; birds and bees and butterflies flocked round him as he labored. He knew what the bees hummed and where they flew to load themselves with honey; butterflies lighted upon his hands and taught him strange things. Birds told him of their travels, and brought him seeds from far countries which he planted in his gardens and which bloomed into marvelous flowers. A swallow who loved him very much and who had seen many wonderful lands once brought him a seed from an emperor's secret garden which none but four of his own slaves had ever seen. These slaves had been born in the garden and would never leave it while they lived.

King Amor planted the seed in a pleasaunce of its own. It grew into the most beautiful blue flower the world had ever known. It was of a blue so pure and exquisitely intense that it was rapture to look at it. Its blossoms hung from a tall stem and in its first year it gave a thousand seeds. Each year Amor planted more flowers and each year they grew taller and more wonderful and blossomed a longer time. When the summer wind blew it shook out clouds of delicate fragrance which sometimes floated down the mountain until the wretched dwellers in King Mordreth's land forgot their quarrels and misery and even lifted their heavy heads to inhale it and ask each other what was being done upon the mountain. Each year King Amor gathered the seeds and stored them in an unused tower of his castle.

Taller and stronger he grew and each day wiser and more beautiful. Each plant, each weed, each four-footed thing, each wind, each star of heaven taught him its wonders and its wisdom. His eyes were so marvelous in their straight-glanced splendor that when he looked at a man they seemed to read his soul and command its truth to answer him. He was so powerful that he could break an iron bar in two pieces with his hands.

When he was twenty years old the Ancient One took him up on the battlements, and giving him a strong glass told him to look down upon the capital city on the plain and see what was being done there.

"I see many people gathered in crowds," Amor said, when he had looked for a few moments. "I see bright colors and waving pennants and triumphal arches. It is as if some great ceremony were being prepared for."

"The people are making ready for your coronation," said the Ancient One. "To-morrow you will be led in state down the mountain and acclaimed King. It was to fit you to reign over your kingdom that I taught you to know all the wonders of the world and have shown you that no thing is useless but folly and dishonoring thought. That which you have learned from your brothers here you go down the mountain to teach your brothers there. You will see things which are not beautiful and those which are unclean, but hold high your head when you walk, young King, and never forget the sun, the wind, and the stars."

To himself as he looked on him the Ancient One said: "When he stands before them they will think he is a young god."

The next morning a splendid procession wound its glittering way up the mountain road to the castle. There were princes and nobles and chieftains. Rich colors glowed in their attire and gorgeous banners and pennants waved over them, while music from gold and silver trumpets accompanied them as they rode and their many followers marched behind.

The Ancient One in his long robe of gray stood by King Amor on the broad stone terrace guarded by its crouching carved lions.

"This is your King, O people!" he said.

And when the people looked it was as he had said it would be. They drew back a little and gazed in fear, and many of the followers fell upon their knees. They thought they saw a beautiful young giant and god. But he was only a splendid and powerful young man who had never known a dark thought and had lived near to his brothers the stars. His horse, adorned with golden trappings, was brought and he was led down the mountain side, through the gates into the capital city of his kingdom. He desired that the Ancient One should ride by his side.

What he saw as he rode to the place of coronation he had never seen before. Notwithstanding the embroidered silk and velvet hangings decorating the fronts of the rich people's houses, he caught glimpses of filthy side streets, squalid alleys, and tumble-down tenements. He saw forlorn little children scud away like rats into their holes as he drew near, and wretched, vicious-looking men and women fighting with each other for places in the crowd. Sharp, miserable faces peered round corners at him, and nobody smiled because every one hated or distrusted his neighbor, and they dreaded and disliked the young King because all the King Mordreths had been evil and selfish, and he was their descendant.

When they saw that he was so tall and powerful and carried his handsome head so high, often looking upward, they feared him still more; as their own heads hung down they never saw anything but the dirt and dust beneath their feet or the quarrels about them, so their minds were full of fears and ugly thoughts, and they at once began to be afraid of him and suspect him of being proud. He could do twice as much evil as the other Kings, they said, since he was twice as strong and twice as handsome. It was their nature to first think an evil thought of anything or anybody and to be afraid of all things at the outset.

The princes and nobles who rode in the procession tried to prevent King Amor seeing the wretched-looking people and ill-kept streets. They pointed out the palaces and decorations and beautiful ladies throwing flowers in his path from the balconies. He praised all the splendors and saluted the balconies, looking up with such radiant and smiling eyes that the ladies almost threw themselves after their flowers and cried out that never, never had there been crowned such a beautiful young King before.

"Do not look at the rabble, your Majesty," the Prime Minister said. "They are an evil, ill-tempered lot of worthless malcontents and thieves."

"I would not look at them," answered King Amor, "if I knew that I could not help them. There is no time to look at dark things if one cannot make them brighter. I look at these because there is something to be done. I do not yet know what."

"There is such hatred in their eyes that they will only make you angry, Sire," said a handsome young prince who rode near.

"There is no time for anger," said Amor, holding his crowned head high. "It is a worthless thing."

After sunset there was a great banquet and after it a great ball, and the courtiers and princes were delighted by the beauty and grace of the new King. He was much brighter and more charming than any of the King Mordreths had been. His laugh was full of gaiety and the people who stood near him felt happier, though they did not know why.

But when the ball was at its height he stepped into the center of the room and spoke aloud to the splendid company.

"I have seen the broad streets and the palaces and all that is beautiful in my capital," he said. "Now I must go to the narrow streets and the dark ones. I must see the miserable people, the cripples, the wretched ones, the drunkards and the thieves."

Every one clamored and protested. These things they had hidden from him; they said kings should not see them.

"I will see them," he said with a smile which was beautiful and strange. "I go now, on foot, and unattended except for my friend the Ancient One. Let the ball go on."

He strode through the glittering throng with the gray-clad Ancient One at his side. He still wore his crown upon his head because he wished his people to know that their King had come to them.

Through dark and loathsome places they went, through narrow streets and back alleys and courts, where people scurried away like rats as the gutter children had done in the daytime. King Amor could not have seen them but that he had brought with him a bright lantern and held it up in the air above his high head. The light shining upon his beautiful face and his crown made him look more than ever like a young god and giant, and the people cowered terrified before him, asking each other what such a King would do to wretches like themselves. But just a few very little children smiled at him because he was so young and bright and splendid. No one in the black holes and corners could understand why a King should come walking among them on the night of his coronation day. Most of them thought that the next morning he would order them all to be killed, and their houses burned, because he would only think of them as vermin.

Once as he passed through a dark court a madman darted out in his path shaking his fist.

"We hate you!" he cried out. "We hate you!"

The dwellers in the court gasped with terror, wondering what would happen. But the tall young King stood holding his lantern above his head and gazing at the madman with deep thought in his eyes.

"There is no time for hatred in the world," he said. "There is no time." And then he passed on.

The look of deep thought was in his face throughout the hours in which he strode on until he had seen all he had come to see.

The next day he rode back up the mountain to his castle on the crag, and when the night fell he lay out upon the battlements under the sky as he had done on so many nights. The soft wind blew about him as he looked up at the stars.

"I do not know, my brothers," he said to them. "Tell me." And he lay silent until the great sweet stillness of the night seemed to fill his soul, and when the stars began to fade he slept in rapturous peace.

The people in his kingdom on the plain waited, wondering what he would do. During the next few days they quarreled and hated each other more than ever, the rich ones because they all wanted to gain his favor, and each was jealous of the other; the poor ones because they were afraid of him and each man feared that his neighbor would betray things he had done in the past.

Only two boys working together in a field, having stopped to wrangle and fight, one of them suddenly stood still remembering something, and said a strange thing in a strange voice:

"There is no time for anger. There

is no time." And as he fell to work again his companion did the same, and when they had finished their task of weeding they talked about the thing and remembered that when they had quarreled the day before they had not finished their task at all, and had not been paid, and had gone home sore from the blows they had given each other, and had had no supper.

"No, there is no time," they decided.

PART III

PART III

AT the beginning of the following week there were rumors that a strange law had been made — the strangest ever known in the world. It was something about a Blue Flower. What had flowers to do with laws, or what had laws to do with flowers? People quarreled about what the meaning of such a law might be. Those who thought first of evil things and fears began to say that in the rich people's gardens was to be planted a Blue Flower whose perfume would poison all the poor.

The only ones who did not quarrel were the two boys and their friends who had already begun to make a sort of password of "There is no time for anger." One of them who was clever added a new idea to the saying.

"There is no time for fear!" he cried out in the field. "Let us go on with our work." And they finished their task early and played games.

At last one morning it was made known that the new King was to give a feast in the open air to all the people. It was to be on the plain outside the city, and he himself was going to proclaim to them the Law of the Blue Flower.

"Now we shall know the worst," growled and shivered the Afraid Ones as they shuffled their way to the plain, and the boys who used the password heard them.

"There is no time to think of the worst!" shouted the clever one at the top of his voice. "There is no time. We shall be late for the feast."

And a number of people actually turned to listen because there was a high, strong, gay sound in his voice such as had never been heard in King Mordreth's Land before.

The plain was covered with thick green grass, and beautiful spreading trees grew on it. There was a richly draped platform for King Amor's gold and ivory chair, but when the people gathered about he stood up before them, a beautiful young giant with eyes like fixed stars and head held high. And he read his law in a voice which, wonderful to relate, was heard by every man, woman, and child — even by the little cripple crouching alone in the grass on the very outskirts of the crowd and not expecting to hear or see anything.

This is what he read:

"In my pleasaunce on the mountain top there grows a Blue Flower. One of my brothers, the birds, brought me its seed from an Emperor's hidden garden. It is as beautiful as the sky at dawn. It has a strange power. It dispels evil fortune and the dark thoughts which bring it. There is no time for dark thoughts — there is no time for evil. Listen to my Law. To-morrow seeds will be given to every man, woman, and child in my kingdom — even to the newborn. Every man, woman, and child — even the newborn — is commanded by the law to plant and feed and watch over the Blue Flower. It is the work of each to make it grow. The mother of the newborn can hold its little hand and make it drop the seeds into the earth. As the child grows she must show it the green shoots when they pierce the brown soil. She must babble to it of its Blue Flower. By the time it is pleased by color it will love the blossoms, and the spell of happiness and good fortune will begin to work for it. It is not one person here and there who must plant the flower, but each and every one. To those who have not land about them, all the land is free. You may plant by the roadside, in a cranny of a wall, in an old box or glass or tub, in any bare space in any man's field or garden. But each must plant his seeds and watch over and feed them. Next year when the Blue Flower blossoms I shall ride through my kingdom and bestow my rewards. This is my Law."

"What will befall if some of us do not make them grow?" groaned some of the Afraid Ones.

"There is no time to think of that!" shouted the boy who was clever. "Plant them!"

. . . .

When the Prime Minister and his followers told the King that larger and stronger prisons must be built for the many criminals, and that heavier taxes must be laid upon the people to rescue the country from poverty, his answer to them was: "Wait until the blooming of the Blue Flower."

In a short time every one was working in the open air, digging in the soil — tiny children as well as men and women. Drunkards and thieves and idlers who had never worked before came out of their dark holes and corners into the light of the sun. It was not a hard thing to plant a few flower seeds, and because the King Amor looked so much more powerful than other men, and had eyes so wonderful and commanding, they did not know what punishment he would invent for them and were afraid to disobey him. But somehow, after they had worked in the sweet-scented earth for a while and had seen others working, the light of the sun and the freshness of the air made them feel in better humor; the wind blew away their evil fancies and their headaches, and because there was so much talk and wondering about the magic of the Blue Flower they became interested, and wanted to see what it would do for them when it blossomed. Scarcely any of them had ever tried to make a flower grow before and they gradually thought of it a great deal. There was less quarreling because conversation with neighbors all about a Blue Flower gave no reason for hard words. The worst and idlest were curious about it and every one tried experiments of his own. The children were delighted and actually grew happy and rosy over their digging and watering and care-taking. Gradually all sorts of curious things happened. People who were growing Blue Flowers began to keep the ground around about them in order. They did not like to see bits of paper and rubbish lying about, so they cleared them away. One quite new thing which occurred was that sometimes people even helped each other a little. Cripples and those who were weak actually found that there were stronger ones who would do things for them when their backs ached, and it was hard to carry water or dig up weeds. No one in King Mordreth's Land had ever helped another before.

The boy who was clever did more than all the rest. He gathered together all the children he could and formed them into a band using the passwords. In time it became quite like a little army. They called themselves The Band of the Blue Flower, and each boy and girl was bound to remember the passwords and apply them to all they did. So, often, when a number of people were together and things began to go wrong, a clear young voice would cry out somewhere like a silver battle cry:

"There is no time for anger!" or "There is no time for hate!" or "There is no time to fret! There is no time."

Among the great and rich people also singular things came to pass. Those who had wasted their days loitering or rioting were obliged to get up in the morning to work in their gardens, and finding that exercise and fresh air improved their health and spirits they began to like it. Court ladies found it good for their complexions and tempers; busy merchants discovered that it made their heads clearer; ambitious students found that after an hour spent evening and morning over their Blue Flower beds they could study twice as long without fatigue. The children of the princes and nobles became so full of work and talk of their soil and their seeds that they quite forgot to squabble and be jealous of each other's importance at Court. Never in one story could it be told how many unusual, interesting, and wonderful things occurred in the once gloomy King Mordreth's Land just because every person in it, rich and poor, old and young, good and bad, had to plant and care for and live every day of life with a Blue Flower. Oh! the corners and crannies and queer places it was planted in; and oh! the thrill of excitement everywhere when the first tender green shoots thrust their way through the earth! And the wave of excitement which passed over the whole land when the first buds showed themselves. By that time every one was so interested that even the Afraid Ones had forgotten to ask each other what King Amor would do to them if they had no Blue Flower. Somehow, people had gained courage and they knew the Blue Flower would grow — and they knew there was no time to stop working while they worried and said "Suppose it didn't." There was no time.

Sometimes the young King was on the mountain top with the wind and the eagle and the stars, and sometimes he was in his palace in the city, but he was always working and thinking for his people. He was not seen by the people, however, until a splendid summer day came when it was proclaimed by heralds in the streets that he would begin his journey through the land by riding through the capital city to see the blossoming of the Blue Flowers, and there would be a feast once more upon the plain.

It was a wonderful day, the air was full of golden light and the sky of such a blueness as never had been seen before. Out of the palace gates he rode and he wore his crown, and his eyes were more brilliant than the jewels in it, and his smile was more radiant than a sunrise as he looked about him, for every breath he drew in was fragrant, every ugly place was hidden, and every squalid corner filled with beauty, for it seemed as if the whole world were waving with Blue Flowers. Tumble-down houses and fences were covered with them because some of them climbed like vines; neglected fields and gardens had been made neat so that they would grow; rubbish and dirt had been cleaned away to make room for clumps and patches of them. You could not grow the Blue Flower among dirt and disorder any more than you could grow it while you were spending your time in drinking and quarreling. By the road sides, in courts, in windows, in cracks, in walls, in broken places in roofs, in great people's gardens, on the window sills, or about the doorways of poor people's hovels — fair and fragrant and waving, grew the Blue Flower. Where it waved there was no room for dirt and rubbish, and suddenly even the dullest people began to see that the face of the whole land was changed as if by some strange magic, and the whole population seemed changed with it. Everybody looked fresher and more cheerful, people had actually learned to smile and keep themselves clean, and there was not one who was not healthier. They had, in fact, been noticing this for some time, and they had said to each other that the power of the Blue Flower, of which the King had spoken, was beginning to work. The children had grown gay and rosy, and the boy who was clever and all his companions had found time to earn themselves new clothes, because they had never forgotten their passwords. All the farmers wanted them to work in their fields because they said there was no time to idle, no time to fight, no time to play evil tricks.

On the King rode, and on and on and on, and the farther he went the more splendid and joyous his smile grew.

But at no time during the day was it more beautiful than when he met the little cripple who had sat on the outside of the crowd on the first feast day, not expecting to see or hear anything.

The cripple lived in a tiny hovel on the edge of the city, and when the glittering procession drew near it the small patch of garden was quite bare and had not a Blue Flower in it. And the little cripple was sitting huddled upon his broken door-step, sobbing softly with his face hidden in his arms.

King Amor drew up his white horse

and looked at him and looked at his bare garden.

"What has happened here?" he said. "This garden has not been neglected. It has been dug and kept free of weeds, but my Law has been broken. There is no Blue Flower."

Then the little cripple got up trembling and hobbled through his rickety gate and threw himself down upon the earth before the King's white horse, sobbing hopelessly and heart-brokenly.

"Oh King!" he cried. "I am only a cripple, and small, and I can easily be killed. I have no flowers at all. When I opened my package of seeds I was so glad that I forgot the wind was blowing, and suddenly a great gust carried them all away forever and I had not even one left. I was afraid to tell anybody."

And then he cried so that he could not speak.

"Go on," said the young King gently. "What did you do?"

"I could do nothing," said the little cripple. "Only I made my garden neat and kept away the weeds. And sometimes I asked other people to let me dig a little for them. And always when I went out I picked up the ugly things I saw lying about — the bits of paper and rubbish — and I dug holes for them in the earth. But I have broken your Law."

Then the people gasped for breath, for King Amor dismounted from his horse and lifted the little cripple up in his arms and held him against his breast.

"You shall ride with me to-day," he

said, "and go to my castle on the mountain crag and live near the stars and the sun. When you kept the weeds from your bare little garden, and when you dug for others and hid away ugliness and disorder, you planted a Blue Flower every day. You have planted more than all the rest, and your reward shall be the sweetest, for you planted without the seeds."

And then the people shouted until the world seemed to ring with their joy, and somehow they knew that King Mordreth's Land had come into fair days and they thought it was the Blue Flower magic.

"But the earth is full of magic," Amor said to the Ancient One, after the feast on the plain was over. "Most men know nothing of it and so comes misery. The first law of the earth's magic is this one. If you fill your mind with a beautiful thought there will be no room in it for an ugly one. This I learned from you and from my brothers the stars. So I gave my people the Blue Flower to think of and work for. It led them to see beauty and to work happily and filled the land with bloom. I, their King, am their brother, and soon they will understand this and I can help them, and all will be well. They shall be wise and joyous and know good fortune."

The little cripple lived near the sun and the stars in the castle on the mountain crag until he grew strong and straight. Then he was the King's chief gardener. The boy who was clever was made captain of his band, which became the King's own guard and never left him. And the gloom of King Mordreth's Land was forgotten, because it was known throughout all the world as The Land of the Blue Flower.

Lightning Source UK Ltd.
Milton Keynes UK
UKOW04f0510201016

285720UK00010B/328/P